FLEUR McHARG

THE
FLOWER
EXPERT

IDEAS AND INSPIRATION
FOR A LIFE WITH FLOWERS

Thames & Hudson

IN MEMORY OF KATE

In a quiet corner of my garden is 'Kate's rose', a tribute to my best friend, who passed away a few years ago after a brave battle with cancer. I rescued the dried rose cutting from the rubbish pile while helping Kate's father sort through her things. Now every year, just before Melbourne Cup week, it blooms the most incredible yellow-centred hot-pink flowers. The scent is unbelievable. I sometimes sit beside this rose bush and talk to Kate, and perhaps give it a drop of gin or some ash from my cigarette.

Kate was wild and fabulous and crazy and fun. I would not be the florist or the person I am today if it weren't for Kate.

FLEUR

was once arrested for stealing magnolias from Como House. I'd noticed a magnificent tree while attending an open day of the historic house and garden with my mother (I was nineteen at the time) and I just knew that I needed to have a branch from it next to my bed. I went back to the garden that evening with a ladder, scaled the fence and snipped a branch. Unfortunately, a conscientious security guard spotted me and phoned the police. My parents were called and had to pay a fine – not to mention suffering the embarrassment of bailing out their criminal daughter. It was all worth it though – I slept with that magnolia branch next to my bed that night.

I've been obsessed with flowers for as long as I can remember. I love the colours, the endless variety of forms and their unique energy. I feel like I was born to work with flowers. (And yes, improbable as it may seem, Fleur is my real name. I'd like to pretend there's some wonderfully glamorous story behind it, but in reality I was named after my mother's dead whippet, Fleur de Lys, who got run over by a car just before I was born. Thanks, Mum.)

As the daughter of milliner Wendy Mead – not to mention the great-niece of British *Vogue* fashion editor Madge Garland – I guess it was inevitable that I would become an artist of some kind. I grew up amid the flurry of my mother's workroom, neck-deep in Valentino satins, Lancetti lace and German Gütermann threads. The night before my Year 12 English exam, I stayed up until 4am helping Mum sew headband ribbons into hats for the Melbourne spring racing carnival. (I passed my exam, by the way.) I often helped my dad to dye fabric for Mum's creations, learning from him how to recreate a colour *exactly* in order to match a particular dress. Immersed in this vibrant world of fashion and creativity, I began a lifelong quest to understand the intricacies of blending and balancing colour.

In Year 10 art, I was asked to paint a self-portrait. All my classmates produced pretty standard, run-of-the-mill portraits. When my teacher, Mr Morrison, came over to look at my work, he was bemused to find that I'd spent the entire session making a wash of different colours, having become completely absorbed in the process of blending the paints. When asked where my self-portrait was, my reply was to quickly sketch a tiny face in the corner of my canvas. Luckily he had a good sense of humour.

For my final year of school, I was among the top six art students in the state. Diana Gold, curator of Gallery 101 in Collins Street, Melbourne, was so impressed with my work that she invited me to create my own exhibition. From there the ball just kept rolling – from art competitions to painting murals for a paint company in Japan. My big break came when I walked into the Como Centre in South Yarra one day, having just returned from backpacking in Europe, and confronted centre management about their hideous Christmas decorations. At the ripe-old-age of 21, and pitted against some huge established companies, I managed to win the tender for creating their next-year's Christmas display. (And, in fact, I did their displays for the following three years.)

A few years later I was asked, somewhat out of the blue, to run a boutique flower shop at the entrance to the revamped Georges Department Store. Opening that shop was the moment I really began to see myself as a florist. I started getting asked to do flowers for weddings, celebrity functions, government events and big fashion brands. The rest, as they say, is history.

For me, every flower has its own unique personality. *The Flower Expert* is a collection of my most-loved flower friends and some of my favourite arrangements, interspersed with stories from my life and work. You'll find information about each flower, as well as plenty of tips and tricks to help you create your own floral masterpieces.

I think my love of flowers stems from, and is inextricably entwined with, the unusual way I understand and perceive colour. I realised when I was quite young that I experience the world differently to most other people. I view and feel everything in life through a lens of colour. Every colour has a unique quality, an individual meaning and feeling associated with it. For example, red is power and strength. My favourite colour is sky-blue: the colour of forget-me-nots, hydrangeas and the summer skies of my childhood. It's a happy colour and I love to wear an element of it most days, because it helps me to feel positive.

Every day of the week has its own colour and character, which influences everything that I do. One of the side effects of this is that I have a really good memory, as moments in time are always linked to particular colours. I can easily recall that a meeting I attended a month ago was on a Tuesday, not a Thursday, because when I think about the meeting I immediately see the colour blue – and Tuesdays are blue, while Thursdays are green.

I've learned that this way of experiencing the world through colour is a form of synaesthesia, a condition that affects sensory perception. Synaesthesia occurs when one sensory pathway involuntarily triggers a different sensory pathway. A common form is when a person perceives letters or numbers as inherently coloured. Synaesthetes often have amazing abilities, like being able to perform complex mental arithmetic or memorise an entire phone book. Often they are very creative and many become involved in visual arts, music or theatre. For me, flowers embody the pinnacle of creative expression.

My daughter is similarly infatuated with colour. When she was three years old, she collected every single pink thing in the house – toothbrushes, toys, cushions – and lined them all up. My mother says I was just the same when I was a child. We both feel an innate need to organise the world by colour.

I think, see and feel everything in colour. Life feels unbalanced if the colours around me are off. So I try to create spaces that 'hum' for me in terms of colour. My home is a place of solace and peace, a refuge from the frenetic colour mash-up of the outside world. The house has a country farm feel, snuggled in a rambling Edna Walling garden. There's a park right next door, so from the house the green seems to stretch for acres. The garden has a life of its own. There are trees covered with ivy, an orange tree that fruits all year round, stephanotis vines trailing up the verandah, and jonquils that have escaped their pots and bloom every year wherever they please. Roses and hydrangeas jostle for space with agapanthus and jasmine in a rowdy free-for-all. Our three dogs (two blue heelers and a kelpie) tear around after each other in endless games of chasey.

As for the house itself: the interior walls are all white, which, along with the high ceilings and large windows, creates a feeling of lightness, clarity and simplicity. The beds are dressed with French linen, also in white. Then there are lots of brown elements (timber floors and furniture), for grounding and cosiness. And of course there are books in every room.

In winter I always have woolly blankets draped over the backs of our lounge chairs and a fire burning in the grate. In spring, I throw open up the windows to let in light and fresh air, and add vibrant green elements to the indoors with vases of newly sprouting branches (Japanese maple is a favourite). Flowers, of course, are the ultimate tool for reflecting the changing seasons. If I'm having people over, I'll pick whatever's blooming in the garden: perhaps camellias or hellebores in winter; white clivias or jonquils in spring; and masses of agapanthus and hydrangeas in summer.

MONDAY

O
R
A
N
G
E

I don't like orange, to be honest, which is probably why I associate it with Mondays – nobody likes Mondays. Orange is a very unflattering colour and Monday is a very unflattering day! Orange can have a harsh, heavy feeling; however, it can also be warm and sunny. It's about the shades you choose. Orange Mondays jolt me out of the weekend and into the start of something new, whether I like it or not.

TUESDAY

B

L

U

E

Blue is my favourite colour and Tuesday is my favourite day. On Tuesdays I tend to feel peaceful, relaxed and safe. The rude shock of Monday is over and I'm beginning to get into the swing of the working week. I don't feel rushed, yet I can get a lot of planning done for the rest of the week.

WEDNESDAY

W
A
T
E
R
M
E
L
O
N

Wednesday's colour is bright and pungent: midway between Monday's orange and Friday's red. The week is starting to get a bit more chaotic and anxiety can start seeping in. It's a day to put my head down and work hard to get boxes ticked and problems solved.

THURSDAY

G

R

E

E

N

Green is another of my favourite colours; it is intrinsically linked with the natural world and has a quiet serenity. On Thursday, the mad rush of Wednesday is over and there's no more planning I can do. This is the day I take a breath and regroup before the Friday marathon begins. It's still a busy working day, but I feel calm and in control.

FRIDAY

R

E

D

Friday arrives with a bang – it reminds me I'm alive! Red is safe, comfortable and strong, so Friday is usually a really productive day, where all the elements of the work I've been preparing over the week come together. However, it is always a flat-out race to the finishing line.

SATURDAY

Y
E
L
L
O
W

Yellow has lightness, freshness and energy. Saturday is the day most of our big events are held, including weddings, so I need all the positivity and energy I can get! This is usually a super-busy day, but also super-fun and satisfying when things go to plan.

SUNDAY

B

R

O

W

N

Brown is grounding and cosy, like a big bear hug. Sunday is my day to spend at home with family, relaxing – preferably in front of an open fire, with a dog at my feet and a glass of wine in my hand.

MY
FLOWER
FRIENDS

or me, flowers are like people: each has its own character, attributes and flaws. I think it all began when I was a young child; I always associated my grandmother with her violet talcum powder. Violets have been a comforting, maternal presence for me ever since.

The rose is the undisputed queen of flowers: stylish, sophisticated and true of heart. The frangipani, on the other hand, is a strumpet: flashy, overly perfumed and a fickle flower. I always think frangipani belongs in Queensland or in Sydney by the harbour. She makes an entertaining summer holiday fling, but she's certainly not the kind of girl you bring home to meet the parents in Melbourne!

By the same token, I associate people with certain flowers. I can immediately picture which flowers somebody would have in their home – usually within minutes of meeting them. In my mind Kim Kardashian's house is filled with big gold pots of white phalaenopsis orchids: like her, they're expensive, flashy and narcissistic. Someone grounded, with a deep connection to the earth, might have a small vase of hydrangeas. A person who understands the importance of the little things in life probably picks forget-me-nots from their garden.

I often wonder at the ingenuity of whichever divine entity it was that conceived of and created flowers, with all their hypnotising intricacies and infinite variety of colours and forms. So often, people don't realise just how exceptional flowers are or give them the respect they deserve. 'Please, people!' I sometimes feel like shouting, 'Just take a moment to refill the vase!' A little care is all that is needed to coax the best out of your cut flowers.

We've all got our people. These are my people.

R
O
S
E
S

Roses exemplify grace and elegance, and they die gracefully too. Allow the petals to fall gently around the base of the vase – the quiet fading of the flower is part of its beauty.

Rose bushes are generally very hardy and easy to grow. In fact, in the right soil they can spread like weeds.

The rose really is the closest you can get to perfection. She is the high priestess of flowers, embodying meaning, emotion and substance. Roses have been used for centuries to signify love, sorrow and friendship. With an extremely high concentration of essential oils in their petals, some people argue that roses have the highest spiritual vibration of all flowers. Perhaps this explains why we feel such adoration for roses.

I like to work with garden-variety roses such as the hybrid teas, which display that 'typical' rose shape, and the David Austins, which have a flatter flower with swirls of petals and an amazing scent. My favourite David Austin rose has to be the Queen of Sweden; she is just exquisite. I can't stand the send-a-single-rose varieties that teenagers give each other for Valentine's day: they don't open, they don't smell; they're the bogan of roses.

DAHLIAS

Cut dahlias will only last a couple of days. To make the most of them, pick off the back petals as they start dying.

The stems can smell terribly as the flowers begin to die (this lady does not age gracefully!). Try growing them in the veggie patch if you want to enjoy these beauties without the stench.

The dahlia is the sexy, beautiful temptress of the flower world. She makes a hell of a first impression, but she's gone by the time you wake up the next morning.

BOU GAIN VIL LE A

Unfortunately, bougainvillea begins to wilt almost as soon as it is cut.

However, it is a hardy garden plant and produces long-lasting, copious blooms.

Grown against a white-washed wall, bougainvillea makes an incredible backdrop for an outdoor wedding or garden party.

Although native to the tropics of South America, bougainvillea makes me think of holidays in Greece and Spain. The plant's flower-like bracts come in a range of near-fluorescent shades and the cerise and hot-pink varieties seem in perfect harmony with the architecture and sun-kissed landscapes of southern Europe. The less common apricot and white types are better suited to the feeling of Melbourne.

ANE
M
O
N E
S

Anemones last well and can add a touch of sophistication to an arrangement that might otherwise have an overly cottagey feel. For example, add them to a vase with dahlias, hellebores, astilbe and David Austins. The arrangement pictured here also includes snow berries and privet berries.

I really love white anemones with a black centre. Unfortunately they can be hard to come by in Australia, so I often buy the more common white anemones with a green centre and paint the inside black. Try it – no one will guess your secret!

BL
O
S S
OMS

Blossoms last well and can be mixed with almost any flower.

Once the flower has finished don't throw out the branches as when left in water they sprout green shoots.

The appearance of blossom is a welcome signal that winter is almost over and spring is on its way. A single pink blossom tree against a blue sky is a sight to see. Even more awe-inspiring is the blossoming en masse of certain stone-fruit trees – the spectacular display of spring cherry blossoms in Japan draws thousands of tourists every year. I love the fluffy blossoms of apple and cherry blossom trees.

MAG
NO
LI
A
S

Magnolias are so magnificent
that they deserve to be
presented on their own;
one large branch in a massive
vase or bucket is all you need.

White magnolias against a
white wall make a bold, elegant
statement. Simplicity is the key.

The white southern magnolia will
only last a day once cut. However,
the pink lily magnolia and saucer
magnolia both last well.

Magnolia is a real southern belle, the epitome of cultivated beauty and charm. In winter in Melbourne, the pink magnolias put on the most amazing show and they're so completely mesmerising I have to be careful not to crash my car.

PE
O
N
IE
S

Peonies combine well with other
pretty flowers. Depending on the
season, I might mix them with
lilac, guelder rose or azalea. Of
course, these blousy ladies also
do perfectly well all on their own.

Pairing white peonies with
dark foliage creates a dramatic,
Dutch Masters-type feel.

Flowers are like babies: the fatter the better. Peonies are
gorgeous, plump and fluffy – which is perhaps why almost every bride I meet requests peonies.
My favourite is the Coral Charm variety, which slowly fades from coral to white. One arrangement
I created for a photo shoot took two weeks to prepare, as I had to wait for the peonies to fade to
the perfect combination of tones.

PLUM
FO
LI
A
GE

Unlike its colour rival, the copper beech, the purple-leaf plum has really strong branches with wonderful shapes. It is a perfect foliage for floral arrangements.

Plum foliage adds a touch of drama and old-world class to any arrangement. It can be matched with almost any flower, from roses to peonies, water lilies to gardenias.

Plum trees grow on nature strips everywhere so it's easy to forage for branches. Pop on a fluoro safety vest and nobody will look twice!

Purple-leaf plum trees can be found lining streets all over Melbourne. They are popular for their bountiful pale-pink blossoms, which brightly herald the arrival of spring, and the amazing colour of their leaves. The spectactular deep-reddish-purple foliage can transform a bunch of flowers you might find in supermarket into one worthy of gracing Harrods, London. It's like slipping into a little black dress: instant glamour!

WA TER LI LI ES

Water lilies must be coerced into staying open. You can snap the outside petals until they crack, or alternatively drip some candle wax into the centre of the flower to hold it open. On the other hand, they can also look quite beautiful when closed.

These water sprites like to bathe in water right up to their chins. Place the flowers in a long-necked vase, which provides plenty of support for their weak, hollow stems.

When selecting water lilies, gently prise open a flower to peek inside – if the centre of the flower shows any sign of turning black, don't buy them, as they're beginning to die.

Water lilies inevitably bring to mind Monet's Impressionist paintings and it's easy to understand the artist's obsession with these stellar beauties. Like their cousin, the sacred lotus, there is something divine about water lilies, with their bright-pink centres fading to pale pink at the edges, the petals perfectly complemented by their bed of dirty-chartreuse-green leaves. They have an air of history about them but, unlike roses, which will always have a nostalgic quality, water lilies can be made to feel fresh and modern.

RA NUN CU LU S

The stems of cut ranunculus start to smell very quickly. However, just as a daily shower can tame one's troublesome BO problem, so too can a daily change of vase water minimise the stink of rotting flower stems – and help the flowers last longer too.

Ranunculus are like a modern, low-maintenance rose. They look good with almost anything and have a contemporary, fresh feel. Young brides love them.

The fluffy and round ranunculus flowers are like a beautiful ballerina's tutu. I can just imagine them lining up to pirouette across the top of a perfectly iced cake. Ranuncs come in an array of colours but the blush-pink variety has to be my favourite – it might just be the perfect flower, if it only had a fragrance.

DOG
WO
OD

Display a large branch of dogwood by itself in a heavy vessel, or combine smaller branches with other spring flowers in an arrangement.

Pink dogwood makes a delicate spring bouquet.

Dogwood is mental. In a good way! I love the individuality of the flowers, the curls of the petals – like a curious snail peeking out of its house. I've never seen dogwood trees in Australia like I saw growing in the in California. I was coordinating an event at an upmarket resort. (FYI it is *the* place to stay. Obama stays there. Everyone stays there.) There were these incredible dogwood trees all over the estate. The head of guest services gave us permission to cut some branches for the exclusive dinner party we were organising. The next day I bought two dogwood trees from the nursery to thank him. The trees were planted in the resort grounds and bear a plaque in my name. Does that make me famous?!

LILY
OF
THE
VALLEY

A bouquet of lily of the valley requires no accompaniment – some flowers shine clearest when left to themselves.

Lily of the valley immediately conjures up an image of my favourite bride ever: Grace Kelly. She played the role of Hollywood actress meets real-life princess better than anyone else ever could have. Everything about her wedding reflected her authenticity and style. It was bona fide glamour, rather than Hollywood glitz: the jewels were real. That woman was all class, from her bone structure to the way she carried herself. As she walked down the aisle, she held a bouquet of lily of the valley that was so elegant yet understated. Every woman and her dog has tried to recreate that bouquet, but not many have managed to replicate the lightness and delicacy of Kelly's. The dainty, unpretentious yet so stylish lily of the valley is the perfect example of true elegance.

FO X GLO VE S

Foxglove leaves quickly go yellow, so peel them off before putting the flowers in a vase.

These flowers look best by themselves in a big bunch, but can also be added to arrangements to create height.

The most well-known foxgloves are the herbaceous or shrubby varieties. But I just love the foxglove (or empress) tree, which, although it belongs to a different plant family, has very similar flowers. The little town of Bright, nestled in the foothills of the Victorian mountains, is home to an avenue of the most stunning foxglove trees I've ever seen. Against the chocolate brown of the branches, the bluey-purple flowers seem almost fluorescent.

GAR
DE
NI
A

The gardenia is the epitome of a bedside-table flower, elegant and sweet-scented.

Gardenia is an irascible flower: touch the petals too much and they will bruise and turn brown.

Because the blooms don't like to be touched, they make an incredibly high-maintenance wedding bouquet. For brides who insist on them, I use special plastic guards to protect the petals from being damaged.

To stop gardenias from going yellow, spray them with salt water; it will extend their life by a day or so. (That said, their odour actually gets even better when they start going yellow.)

Gardenia is the elegant yet slightly neurotic grande dame of the flower world. An eccentric lady, she likes to have people around her, but doesn't like to be touched. The heady, intoxicating smell of gardenia reminds me of my mum, of Sydney and balmy summer nights.

SW EET PE A S

Sweet peas are at their sweetest when presented by themselves.

Like most cut flowers, they will last best during the middle of the flowering season, rather than at the beginning or end.

I love the twisted tendrils of sweet peas, and their soft, delicate smell. The name is perfect – how could such a charming flower be named anything else? The pale blush-pink ones are particularly beautiful.

HEL LE BO RES

To help hellebores last, scald the bottom of the stems in boiling water for 20 seconds, then plunge them into cold water (the stems will change from green to a brownish colour).

Hellebores are winter flowers, they like the cold – they won't do well in a heated indoor space.

When selecting hellebores, look at the thickness of the stem near the flower. A thin stem won't hold the weight of the flower head and it will soon flop over.

Hellebores are easy to grow. I plant them under hydrangeas, whose foliage protects them from the sun in summer. When the hydrangeas are cut back in winter, the hellebores come into their own.

Often known as winter roses, these dainty, fragile-looking little flowers come in a wonderful variety of colours – I particularly love the double ones and the insane black ones. They are rather old-fashioned, perhaps something that your mother used to grow, and they do fondly remind me of my childhood. I grow some amazing bright green ones in my own garden. People often think cut hellebores don't have much stamina, but if treated correctly they can survive well.

GUEL
DER
ROSE

Guelder rose and lilac form an amiable partnership for any occasion.

For weddings, guelder roses make a refined bridal posy and are beautiful on a table mixed with other flowers. For a young bride getting married at a traditional venue, I might create a bouquet of guelder roses mixed with peonies and traditional roses, incorporating pale pinks and pistachio. For a wedding ceremony in a grand old house, I might decorate with masses of guelder roses heaped in antique wicker baskets.

Guelder roses have woody stems. Your grandmother may have taught you to split the stems so it's easier for the water to get up, but a bash with a hammer or mallet is actually more effective (and satisfying to boot).

I wanted to get married in October but couldn't because I was marrying a grazier and spring is shearing time. If I *had* had a spring wedding I certainly would have invited the supremely elegant and sophisticated guelder rose to the party. When I enter a room hosting a bevy of these flowers, I know that whoever lives in this house has some serious style. Guelder rose can also be known as snowball viburnum.

RHO
DO
DEN
DRONS

Rhododendron branches can be quite asymmetrical and elegant, and display well just by themselves.

Rhododendrons look best with most of their leaves removed.

Many people dismiss rhododendrons as antiquated, so they're not easy to buy nowadays. Sadly there aren't many growers specialising in the more unusual and less popular flower varieties. Personally, I like the brightness and fluffiness of rhodos. Luckily you can still find them in plenty of suburban backyards.

POP
PI
ES

Poppies like to have their stems scalded in boiling water or flamed briefly before being put into cold water.

You can encourage a closed bud to open by gently peeling off the outer casing.

Do you remember Clinkers? Oh the delightful anticipation of that moment just before you chomp through the chocolate shell, wondering what colour the inside will be this time. Poppies are the Clinkers of the flower world, because you never know what you're going to get until they open. I love peeling open the buds to reveal the crinkled petals hiding inside. I adore the quirkiness of poppies, with their crumpled-paper-like flowers and squiggly stems all akimbo. Their imperfection is perfection to me.

DEL
PHI
NI
UM

Delphinium can add height to a large arrangement of mixed flowers, but also looks amazing by itself in a huge bunch.

The bright and pale blues of delphinium make a bold statement against a green background. I once styled a state dinner for visiting royalty using nothing but massive vases of delphiniums to contrast with the green carpet of the hall. The effect was majestic.

Delphinium is so classically British; it reminds me of Beatrix Potter's tales of Peter Rabbit. I imagine it growing in Mr McGregor's stone-walled cottage garden, alongside hollyhocks, stocks and lupins (and radishes and lettuces, of course). The 'Princess Caroline' variety (shown here) has the most extraordinary coral colour.

AU
TU
MN
FO
LI
AGE

I like to mix branches of different varieties, using whatever I have to hand. Any autumn foliage will do, but rosehip and dogwood are perhaps my favourites.

With autumn arrangements, it's all about creating texture. There's no need for flowers, as the leaves provide all the colour you need.

I often arrange autumn branches in big old wooden buckets. The Bayeux-tapestry colours of the leaves blend beautifully with my antique oak furniture. It feels a little like living in a 16th-century English manor.

I adore autumn. The changing colour of the leaves is such a lovely reminder that the season of cosiness is upon us, that it's time to snuggle in front of log fires on lazy Sunday afternoons. Autumn foliage has such rich, earthy tones; it gives me this scrumptious feeling, like that contentment that comes from smelling freshly baked bread. I love to fill my house with big branches of leaves in autumn; it makes me feel like I could be anywhere in the world. (My husband is not so warmed by them, as the leaves drop all over the floor.)

CYM BI DI UM OR CHI DS

You can quite easily grow cymbidium orchids in pots under trees in your garden. They don't need much water and they keep sprouting back year after year.

Bring potted orchids inside while they're blooming, or snip sprigs of flowers to display in a vase. When the display has finished, throw the pots back outside and don't even look at the plants for a year.

These proud ladies thrive on neglect. Well, they do in my garden...

The cymbidium orchid is a gracious old dame, full of character and substance. There is something of a European feel about these orchids and they have a beautiful slight fragrance. They look rather grand planted in large pots en masse indoors, tucked up against the bones of a lovely old house. For a modern house, on the other hand, a stem or two in a vase on a sideboard is more suited.

DA PH NE

Arranging daphne doesn't require any tricks. Just pop a single sprig in a little vase.

A tub of daphne outside the front door is a wonderful way to welcome visitors.

Daphne can be a little temperamental and is fussy about her growing conditions – she doesn't like too much frost, or too much water (or too little) – but when she's happy, you can smell it.

The charisma of daphne is not in how it looks, but in its incomparable scent: daphne smells like Froot Loops taste. Not even the world's best perfumiers have managed to bottle the sweet, heady aroma of this winter flower. Scent is such a powerful trigger for memory; the perfume of a certain flower can bring back a particular moment with intense clarity. For that reason, I feel daphne should always be used if you are getting married in winter – for the rest of your life its smell will transport you back in time to your happiest day. Because I am always so taken with the scent of daphne, I rarely stop to take a photo. Here it is hidden in this crate of flowers.

PA
PER
DAI
SIES

Paper daisies look best by
themselves; a big bunch in
a single colour is just lovely.
However, they can be used
judiciously in arrangements
where they match the tone of
the other flowers – for example,
pink paper daisies mixed with
pink water lilies and dahlias.

Daisies are my mum's favourite flower. I think of daisies
as sweet, innocent little girls. Perhaps it's their lack of pretention that causes them to often be
overlooked nowadays. I love the variety and depth of colour that you see in paper daisies: the
maroons, deep reds, and bright pinks and oranges, while the white ones have a creamy silveryness
that's enchanting.

JAS
MI
NE

These unpretentious flowers
with their gorgeous scent
make a beautiful bedside
or bathroom decoration.
Plop them in a jam jar: a simple
vessel for a simple flower.

Once the flowers die off on the
vine or shrub, the leaves still look
nice in a vase. I like to pay tribute
to the plant's natural tendancies
by arranging stems in a lovely
long trail.

The scent of jasmine is the first sign of spring, bringing with it
that delightful feeling that winter is finally over. Like burning autumn leaves and freshly cut grass,
it's a smell that brims with nostalgia. As a child I used to pick the flowers from the vines and suck
the nectar out of the bottom. Smelling jasmine now takes me straight back to those halcyon days
of my youth.

HY DRA NG E AS

Hydrangeas look wonderful en masse. Unlike most flowers, they suit any style of architecture, complementing a modern house just as well as a period home.

I also love them in a garden, watching the elegant way they change colour in autumn.

Hydrangeas make an excellent base and filler. I like to use them as a scaffold for building bouquets and vase arrangements. They also make lovely dried arrangements.

Give hydrangea stems a good bash before placing them in a vase. They also like drinking from their heads, so to refresh them spray generously with water or even give them a good dunking.

In the late 1990s, when Stephen Bennett and Sir Terence Conran were attempting to revive Melbourne's Georges department store in Collins Street, I was employed to assist their visual merchandiser and stylist, Louella Potter, who was fresh off the plane from England. I picked her up at 3am to take her on a tour of the local flower market. As we strolled along, I commented on some 'divine' hydrangeas. Louella was taken aback – in England hydrangeas were considered to be hopelessly old-fashioned. 'In Britain, we love gerberas,' she stated. Little did she know that I wouldn't touch a gerbera if you paid me. After that rocky start, Louella and I became firm friends. And now she loves hydrangeas almost as much as I do. I mean, who couldn't fall in love with the fullness, the fatness, the simplicity of hydrangeas?

BR AN CH E S

One great branch in a heavy vessel is all you need. Simplicity is everything.

Choose a branch that has a sense of movement. A little stem won't cut it: you want a decent-sized branch with plenty of offshoots.

If you remember to top up the vase now and then, leafy branches will last for ages.

Branches of green foliage make a house feel fresh and vital. Unless it's a special occasion, I choose to prettify my living areas with greenery rather than vases of flowers. Any kind of branch will do – just pick whatever you have in the garden – but some of my favourites are Japanese maple, oak and loquat.

IT'S
ALL
ABOUT
THE
BASE

My philosophy for creating flower arrangements is always the same, whether I'm decorating my own home or working for a client: let the flower be the star. People so often try to push flowers into unnatural forms. My belief is that when it comes to beauty, you can't beat nature. Let the flower be what it is meant to be. Work with the natural form of a branch, allowing it to bend and twist as it did on the tree, rather than forcing it into an artificial shape.

One of my biggest inspirations is the work of legendary London florist Constance Spry. Spry believed in working with the natural shape of a flower. If a branch or stem naturally inclined to one side, she allowed it to lean that way. She was also a master of finding beauty in whatever she had to hand. She caused quite a stir in the 1930s when she began using weeds, hedgerow plants and vegetables in her arrangements. She was a true innovator, creating the most beautiful designs using an eclectic array of materials from the natural world. Trends in floristry and design come and go, but the style of Constance Spry is truly timeless.

My design style is a modern-day reinterpretation of old-school knowledge. Granted that, I think it's important to reinvent oneself constantly, to be adaptable. My arrangements are always going to have a 'Fleur' bent, but some will be more modern, some more classic. I'm continuously adapting my approach to suit the particular client and space I'm working with.

The first step to working with flowers in an artful way is to recognise that the beauty of every branch and stem is unique and transient. We have to be open to working with the flowers we have in front of us. Give the flower its moment. People often try to trick things up too much, they overthink and overwork things. Let the flower be the flower.

Where the true skill of the florist comes into play is when you are assessing the colours and tones of the flowers you have to work with. You have to trust your instinct and be guided by that. Let go of the fear. I think many people are born with creativity, but are held back from expressing it because they are intimidated or fear failure. If we let go of self-doubt, there's no limit to the things we can achieve.

If I could give any advice to a young florist just starting out, it would be this: your work must stand for itself. It's not enough to have an Instagram account and 10,000 followers. The smoke and mirrors of marketing and PR can only get you so far. In a service industry like this, you're only ever as good as your last job. There's a lot to be said for old-fashioned business acumen. If you are good at what you do, and you do right by the people you work for, you won't need to market yourself – the clients will come to you. Many of the floral arrangements featured in this book were designed for well known people of one kind or another. In most cases, I have chosen not to name names. This is partly because my clients expect and rely on my discretion, but mostly because I whole-heartedly believe that it's not who you work for; it's the work you do.

IT
BEGINS
WITH
THE
VESSEL

People may be shocked to learn that a good florist begins by choosing the vessel and *only then* decides which flowers will be used. It's no good choosing fabulous flowers only to discover that you don't have the right vase to hold them.

A florist should be able to look at any vase and know what could go in it. Begin by looking at the height of the vase, the weight of it, the size and shape of the opening and body. Try to picture what type of arrangement it might hold. Should (and could) this vase hold tall straight stems, tangled asymmetric branches, or perhaps a tightly bunched posy?

Of course, it is inevitable that in some instances we will have to select a vase to suit the flowers available to us. In such cases, the process works in reverse. I once used a dog bowl as a vase when working with a very successful ceramic designer. Artists are so intent on designing beautiful objects that they quite often forget about functionality. On this occasion, the client had provided me with an array of his beautiful ceramic vases to work with, but they all had skinny openings. A florist can't do much with a skinny opening; we need a wide mouth in order to create a solid base and full-bodied floral arrangement. Luckily, the dog bowl I managed to pilfer from his canine companion made a perfect vessel for my flowers.

When using a bottle as a vase, balance is the most important thing. Ensure you balance the width and height of the arrangement, while creating a natural flow.

For a tall branch of flowers, such as magnolia, choose a large vessel with a narrow opening, like a big medicine jar. The vessel must be heavy enough once full of water to support the weight of the branch, while the opening must be slim enough to keep it upright.

A
GOOD
BASE

Once you have decided on your vase and the flowers you'll be using, you must figure out whether you will need to create a base of foliage – and if so, what kind of base?

A base is like a primer. It's the oh-so-important preparation you do at the very beginning to ensure the final result looks exactly as you desire – and that it will last. The base of a floral arrangement is usually made with foliage, arranged in such a way as to offer a sturdy foundation for your flowers. Many florists rely on floral foam to anchor their stems, but this can result in arrangements that lack depth and it also restricts the type of vessel you can use. Understanding how to build a sturdy base of foliage grants you the freedom to create the shape you want, in the vase you want.

Using foliage is not the only way to create a base. I like to use hydrangeas as a base for bouquets and floral arrangements as it looks lovely and complements almost any variety of flower.

Basing is perhaps the most technically difficult aspect of floristry, because it is different every time. The key is being able to visualise what the finished arrangement will look like and work backwards from there. Look at the shape of each stem and go with that, don't try to force it in another direction. Also try to predict what could go wrong, considering the final position of the vase and how it will be transported, and design the base to cope with those factors. A good base guarantees *nothing* will ruin your arrangement.

HOW TO CREATE A

FOLIAGE BASE

I always use a foliage base to anchor an arrangement in a vase. It's a beautiful, natural way to give structure and shape to flowers for a special occasion. You can make a foliage base out of most kinds of foliage.

The leaves must, first and foremost, complement the colours of your flowers. The foliage must also possess the right characteristics to best support the flowers, so consider the shape of the leaves (large/small, long/short), the arrangement of the leaves on the branch (close together/spread out), and the thickness and shape of the stems (soft/woody, straight/twisted).

Begin adding foliage to your vessel one branch at a time, trimming the stems to size as you go and putting in the shortest pieces first. Weave the stems together in a criss-cross pattern to create a strong lattice foundation, while ensuring the foliage forms the shape you have in your mind.

Start adding your flowers to the arrangement one at a time. If you find the base is not strong enough to support the flowers or is visually the wrong shape, take the flowers out and adjust the foliage before continuing.

In the picture opposite, the whole table arrangement is created with a foliage base. I used long trough vases packed with green foliage. In this instance, the foliage drapes beautifully and also provides great support for the roses and other flowers dotted throughout.

HYDRANGEAS AS A BASE

Cut the stems of your hydrangeas to the height of the vase: the head of each hydrangea should rest on the lip of the vase, while the base of the stem sits on the bottom of the vase.

Position the hydrangeas so that the heads are close together – this creates a firm foundation for the rest of your flowers and stops foliage from going in the water.

Strip the leaves from the bottom part of each flower stem, then slide them, one-by-one, between the hydrangea florets to create your arrangement. (This technique can also be used to build a bouquet.)

HOW TO CREATE A
VASE ARRANGEMENT

Choose the vase first and then the flowers.

Decide from which angle the vase will be seen.

Start by creating a sturdy base, using one or more types of foliage. Soft, small-leaved foliage is best for vases.

Once you have a good base, you can start adding flowers to create height and depth.

Stems should be cut on an angle (particularly when using floral foam) so the flowers have more surface area to drink from.

Flowers should sensitively reflect their surroundings and not be too over the top. They should complement the décor, rather than compete with it.

It is generally better to have odd numbers of flowers.

Vase arrangements should have a sense of movement, so let the stems lean naturally.

Leave some space between the foliage and flowers.

When positioning a cluster of vases, place the tallest or largest vessel in the centre.

HOW TO
PEEL A ROSE

A 'peeled' rose has a fullness and sumptuousness that is completely different to a rose that has not been opened. I think they look spectacular and often I use peeled South American hybrid tea roses for glamorous occasions. A large event, like a wedding, might require 4000 roses and it takes about a minute to peel each one. It's not uncommon to walk into our warehouse in Murrumbeena to find six or seven women sitting around frantically peeling roses for a wedding that's happening the next day.

There is definitely an art to peeling a rose – it's a delicate process and you don't want to create sharp edges or a protruding centre. Here's how I do it.

Allow roses that have been refrigerated to come to room temperature before you begin, otherwise the petals will tear.

Fold back the outside petals one by one, using your thumb to support the base of the petal where it meets the stem.

Touch the petal as little as possible, to avoid creating any hard creases.

Roll your fingers gently around the sides of the petal to fold the edges under slightly and smooth it into place.

Continue peeling petals until only a small bud remains in the centre of the flower.

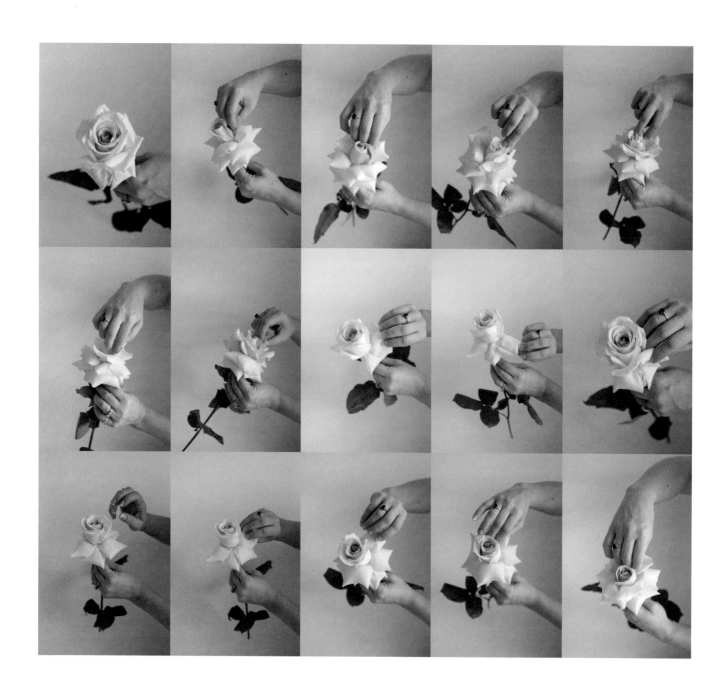

COLOUR
IS
MY
LANGUAGE

or a florist, as for any artist, the ability to understand and balance colour is paramount. Colour blending is a real skill and one of the hardest elements of floristry to do well. It's also very difficult to teach. Colour is about tones and hues and shades. I say to my team, you have to feel the ups and the downs of the arrangement, just as you might feel a piece of music. There has to be emotion in it. I have an innate colour confidence, which I think comes from the intense relationship I've had with colour my whole life. Colour is my native language. A colour combination that someone else may find to be too risky can feel very natural for me. I have learned that I can always trust my instincts. There is an element of science to it, but by-and-large it's an intuitive process.

To create a well-blended arrangement, you first need to comprehend the science behind colour. First off, colours can be divided into 'hots' and 'cools': hot colours are the pinks, reds, oranges and yellows; cool colours are the blues, greys, purples and greens. In general, hots and cools should be kept separate.

These two groups can be further broken down into tonal sub-categories. When it comes to pink, for example, there are the mauve-based pinks, the blue-based pinks, the orange-based pinks and the red-based pinks. Reds can be blue-based or orange-based.

As a framework for blending colour, it's useful to organise the various tones into three broad groups: pastels, bright pastels, and brights. Then there's just one rule to remember: pastels can blend with bright pastels, and bright pastels can blend with brights, but brights and pastels should *never* mix.

Once you understand these basic ideas, you can begin to see how colours should – and should not – be blended.

Of all the fashion designers, Giorgio Armani has by far the best eye for tonal colour. Yves Saint Laurent and Christian Lacroix may be adventurous, but Armani truly *understands* colour. His use of colour is subtle and beautiful, combining taupes with browns and beautiful greys: grey upon grey upon grey. He is a true master.

The first step to blending is to pick the flower you want to be the focal point of your arrangement. Then you need to find the tones that complement and best showcase that star flower. Unfortunately, nature can't replicate a Pantone chart, so to get the colour combination perfect, you *have* to blend.

Imagine you are an artist who needs to mix the perfect paint colour: you need to know which basic elements make up that particular shade and in what proportions. If you don't have a lot of experience working with colour, playing with paints is a fantastic way to learn. Take your colour sample and your paints outside into the natural light and experiment with mixing colours until you achieve the perfect match.

When I'm teaching my team about colour mixing, I sometimes ask them to think about how they blend their eye shadow. If you have a dark brown close to your eyelashes, you might blend in a lighter shade above to lift it. It's the same with flowers: you can use shades of pink to accentuate dark-burgundy flowers, for example.

As you learn more about colour, you will find there are certain adages that begin to ring true: blue and green should never be seen without something in between, for example. Let nature be your mentor: you need only look out the window to see that blues (the sky) and browns (the earth) are natural compatriots.

COLOUR
TREE

BLUE BASED

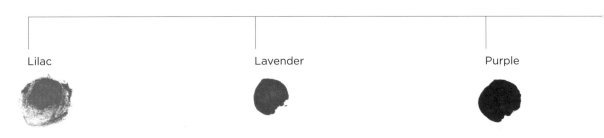

Lilac

Lavender

Purple

RED BASED

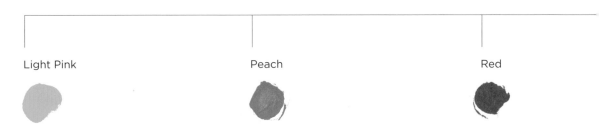

Light Pink

Peach

Red

YELLOW BASED

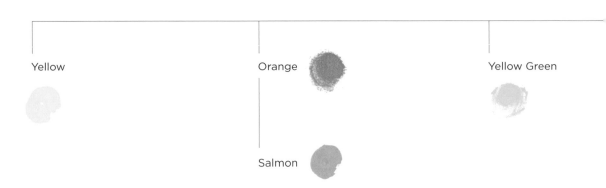

Yellow

Orange

Yellow Green

Salmon

Light Blue
Sky Blue

Dark Blue

Blue Green

Dark Green

Burgundy

Red Orange

Coral

Green

Light Green

Turquoise

PASTEL WEDDING

Pastels are the colours that occur most in nature; just look to the sea, earth and sky for inspiration. For the wedding in this picture, we were given a single piece of ribbon around which the colour scheme was to be built. It was a complex lilac-taupe-mushroom-mauve sort of colour, and certainly not a colour that could be matched by a single naturally occurring flower. To create arrangements that would 'match' the ribbon, I blended three different roses together: white, taupe and pale apricot. In unison, the trio of colours perfectly complemented the ribbon.

PASTEL VASE

In this pink and white arrangement (at left), I've created the pure-pastel feel by toning down the lolly pinks with muted brown tones. The beige/taupe colour of the oncidium orchids is repeated in the bundle of ribbons.

TRADITIONAL PASTELS

This vase arrangement of phalaenopsis orchids, peonies, and euphorbia is an example of a perfectly balanced traditional pastel arrangement. It celebrates the classic partnership of pink, pistachio and white. The copper vase gives it a modern edge.

PASTEL BOUQUET

For a wedding bouquet, it's hard to go past David Austin roses and peonies. The geranium leaves provide texture and fragrance.

PASTEL ORCHIDS

When the extremely talented Amanda Henderson from Gloss Creative came to me with her design for the Melbourne Cup, I knew straight away that not just any flower would work with her simple yet seriously sophisticated design. I chose to focus on the colour pops within her design and use those colours by choosing one flower – phalaenopsis orchids – en masse, dyed exactly the same as the pops in the marquee. The result was incredible.

PASTELS WITH DEEP TONES

In this example, I've blended pastels with darker flowers in matching tones. If I'd mixed the plum-coloured magnolias with cerise-pink flowers, for example, it would have killed the pastel of the pale-pink rose. Instead, I chose flowers in colours that don't fight each other for attention: pale-pink ranunculus and astilbe, with mid-tone pink stock, azalea and cherry blossom. The green hydrangeas and hellebores provide a delicate balancing tone. Adding an element of black to pastels, as I have here, can take an arrangement from girlish to refined.

BLOCK PASTELS

Here I have balanced super-dark burgundies on one side of the arrangement with super-light pastels on the other. It works because of the careful gradient from the darks to the lights. The keystone is the taupe flower in the centre, which has red flecks through it: it tricks the eye into seeing a blended colour that perfectly bridges the burgundies and pale pinks. That taupe and red combination is repeated in the ribbons, creating a sense of balance and symmetry.

PASTELS
WITH GREY FOLIAGE

If you tried to blend bright- or dark-green foliage
with these pastel blooms, the colours would lose
their pastel tone. The soft grey-green of the leaves
used here complements the pastel tones, rather
than competing with them. Similarly, there is no
way to blend green foliage in with grey foliage
without looking unsophisticated. However, dark-
plum foliage can add a dramatic element to a grey
and pastel arrangement.

PASTELS WITH BRIGHT PASTELS

Here I have used blues and greens from the cool side of the colour chart and combined them with their complete opposite, pink. Usually this colour combination wouldn't work, but in this instance the blue shoes bring a sense of cohesion to the composition: their turquoise colour is a combination of the blue of the delphiniums and the green of the foliage, while the pink exactly matches the centres of the water lilies. The addition of white flowers, such as daisies and jasmine, lightens the arrangement to ensure the shoes stand out.

The designer shoes and clean white background ensure the floral colour combination doesn't look dated. A similar effect could be achieved by placing an arrangement like this on a crisp white tablecloth, with turquoise-blue glassware or napkins in place of the shoes.

LIME POP

In this vase arrangement of roses, hydrangeas, mulberries, delphinium and sedum, it's the lime green that makes the pastels really pop. Put lime green with pastel pink and miraculously the pink transforms into a bright pastel. If I'd used apricot in this arrangement instead of lime, the pink would have been toned down. The addition of the hot-pink waterlillies only works because of those vivid lime tones.

FLARE OF FIRE

All the flowers in this image are from the pink and red colour group. To combine the cooler apricot/peach pastel colours with the bright pinks, I needed to add coral in between. Without the coral tone, the arrangement would look flat.

SPRINGTIME

Spring is the time to style bright pastels.
In this arrangement, I wanted to create
a modern Aussie feel by offsetting the
bright pastel flowers against a blue backdrop.
Because it's a 'hot' arrangement, I chose a
summer-sky blue to make the flowers really
pop. If I'd used a cool china-blue or dark-blue
backdrop, it would have dulled the impact of
the flowers rather than enhancing it.

A SONG OF COLOUR

For this photo shoot I set the bright pastel flowers against a wallpaper featuring rich brown and orange tones. The flower that makes this whole arrangement sing is the pinky-purple magnolia – without that pastel element, the colours would seem dull. In contrast to the bright pastel spring arrangement earlier, this one would have looked awful against a blue backing, because it incorporates warm lemon and orange tones, rather than bright yellow and watermelon. This arrangement has a more sophisticated European feel.

BRIGHT PASTELS WITH BRIGHTS

Bright arrangements can come across as tacky or over-the-top if you're not careful (an arrangement of irises mixed with red gerberas, yellow lilies and hard green foliage is basically my idea of hell). One way to pare back brights is by teaming them with a blue-grey vessel. The cool tone of the vases here also allowed me to add pops of blue in the way of delphiniums, which would otherwise seem misplaced. The softer bright pastels of the pink water lilies and peach David Austins also help to tone down the flamboyance of the brights.

TEQUILA!

The brief from this Brazilian bride was simply to make her wedding as bright as possible. I combined bright colours from the warm side of the colour wheel only: oranges, pinks and reds. The arrangement includes roses, dahlias, ranunculus, cumquats and peonies. To offset the over-the-top colour of the flowers, all the décor at the wedding was plain white.

LET
THE
FLOWER
BE
THE
STAR

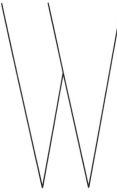

hat I love most about working with flowers is that they are of great importance to people everywhere because they are present at all of our most momentous occasions: births, marriages and funerals. Because flowers are so emotionally evocative, the flowers you choose for these occasions can come to hold a special connection to the event in your memory. Choosing daphne for a winter wedding, for example, means that whenever the couple smell daphne in their later life, it will bring back memories of their wedding. Funeral flowers, on the other hand, can become fondly associated with the memory of the person being farewelled.

When designing flowers for a special event – whether a birthday party, wedding anniversary or second (or third!) wedding – my motivation is always to create floral arrangements that the hosts and their guests will remember for many years to come. Flowers must be appropriate for the client, the occasion, the venue and the season; all these things must be taken into account when selecting blooms, vessels and decor.

When it comes to weddings, unfortunately you can't just pick your favourite Pinterest post and expect your florist to copy it. The flowers need to not only fulfil the wishes of the betrothed, but also suit the season as well as the physical environment.

The best piece of advice I can give to someone planning their wedding is: don't be trendy. Your wedding should have a timeless quality. You want to be a Grace Kelly, not a reality TV star having their fifteen minutes of fame.

Understand that you are planning a wedding, not a party. Social media, WAGs and Pinterest have managed to convince a whole generation that a wedding is just a big party – it's not! Parties can be trendy; parties can be light-hearted and fun.

A wedding should be beautiful, classic and elegant. Which is not to say that your wedding must be traditional or old-fashioned. Just respect that this is a big moment in your life, a day that you will look back on in your memories (and in a lot of photographs!) for decades to come.

Here you will find a selection of favourite floral moments from my life and career. Some of these events ran like clockwork, with the careful hours of foreplanning and preparation leading smoothly and predictably to a wonderful result. However, many of them encountered various unforeseen circumstances – sometimes fortuitous but more often than not calamitous. Funnily enough, it's often the events that don't run to plan that end being the most beautiful, satisfying and of course memorable.

THE
BLUE
DRESS

This photograph is an example of how sometimes our most spontaneous work can turn out to be the best. It was part of a shoot for an editorial feature for Mexican *Vogue*. The brief was to hero the spectacular Tony Maticevski dress. It was a dream collaboration with photographer Sam Bisso, stylist extraordinaire Emily Ward, and make-up queen Victoria Martin.

When I arrived at the set, I found there was no way to attach the flowers to the wall, so I had to create the arrangement on a piece of board that we found on the premises, and then prop that against the wall. The wooden chair we'd planned on using turned out to be far too solid and distracting, so I used a clear plastic stool I happened to find out the back. Once we started shooting, I could see that the foliage I'd brought with me just wasn't dense enough, so I grabbed some lengths of ivy growing on the outside of the building and wove those in. I had chosen a combination of pale-pink roses with blue hydrangeas to complement the delicate hue of the dress, but I ended up removing almost all of the blue flowers, as they were detracting from the dress – in the final version of that main image you can see just the tiniest hint of blue. The last, fortuitous, thing to go wrong that day was that I forgot to sweep the floor; those few fallen rose petals proved to be the icing on the cake.

The picture of Linnea Gröndahl posed in front of a tangled arch of roses and ivy went viral.

PINK
LACE

This is another one of my favourite photo shoots with the dream team from The Blue Dress. The degree of difficulty for this shoot was seriously off the richter scale. We wanted the flowers to look as though they were floating in mid-air. There was one pole at the top and the flowers were woven together. There was nothing behind them.

My team and I stitched orchids, peonies and flowering teatree together, to echo the lace effect of the dress.

NAPA
VALLEY
WINERY

This was the event where everything that could go wrong *did* go wrong. It's a long story (featuring a geriatric chauffeur, an albino butler and a near-death experience) but I'll give you the short version!

Earlier this year I was asked to style an exclusive dinner at a winery in the Napa Valley, California. The venue is a long concrete cavern, intended for storing wine. My idea is to create an authentic Scandinavian feel: pared back, clean and sophisticated. My design incorporates a majestic avenue of trees running along the length of the hall. There is to be lots of light-coloured wood and the tables will be softly lit by wire-framed lanterns, to counteract the stark setting. The cutlery will be sleek and black. I brief an American event team to source all the tableware, plants and ornamentation locally. I will decide on flowers when we get there, depending on what is available. Unfortunately, once we arrive it becomes clear that despite the best efforts of the team something has been lost in translation.

Just hours before the guests are due to arrive, I discover that the 'avenue of trees' I'd requested consists of at least four different types of shrub, all of varying shapes and sizes. Also, the cutlery is pewter, not black. There are no lanterns. To top it all off, the concrete tunnel where we are supposed to be setting up the tables is as cold as the tundra and there's no heating. At this point the host of the event walks in to the freezing, empty cavern and bursts into tears. I decide that I am going to make this event happen or die trying. The next few hours are a blur: ten (matching) maple trees are ordered and delivered, seat warmers bought and rigged up, lighting installed, carpet laid, and spectacular dogwoods purloined from the grounds of a nearby hotel. With minutes to spare, we light the candles and pray that nothing catches fire. We are flustered, sweaty and dirty, but we've done it. And then in saunters a Hollywood A-lister wearing the most exquisite suit you've ever seen … but that's a story for another day.

DUTCH MASTERS STYLE

Throughout history, flowers have been highly valued. Economic markets have risen and fallen on the value of flowers such as tulips and hyacinths. Centuries ago, artists painted flowers because real flowers were so incredibly expensive. Capturing the essence and beauty of a complex living thing like a flower is, however, no easy task. I think that, of all the art movements in history, the painters of the Dutch Golden Age most realistically and sensitively depicted the floral world.

With astonishing realism, the still lifes of the 17th century Dutch Masters capture colour and detail almost as successfully as the human eye. The play of light and shadows gives the flowers a feeling movement and life.

Photographing flowers well is just as difficult as painting them. Occasionally, the right conditions arise to capture an image that is almost on par with those antique masterpieces. This shot of tulips, peonies, roses and fritillaries was taken in the back of our work van, capturing a brief moment in time when the light shining through the back doors created a glorious depth of colour and contrast.

ELEGANT COUNTRY WEDDING

The brief for this country wedding was, 'Not one flower in sight!'. As the ceremony was to be held on a farm, under giant elm trees, I took the bucolic surroundings as my inspiration. I used wheat to create the bride's bouquet and crowns for the flower girls, and cut eucalyptus branches from the property to create arrangements of foliage. I did sneak a few white roses and peonies into the altar arrangements, just to give them some definition.

For the after-party, in a wool shed, I stuck with the rustic theme, adorning the room with lush green foliage – grape vines, gum leaves, olive branches – and placing potted herbs in paper bags on the tables. To create a feeling of luxury amongst all this simplicity, I wrapped hay bales in the most obscenely expensive Scottish linen lace.

It was a very emotional time for this family and when the bride's mother arrived, she told me, 'I wouldn't change a thing'. There were more than a few teary eyes that day.

POTTING
SHED
WEDDING

This wedding was all about creating a feeling of luxury amongst the most simple of settings, maintaining a casual air while still feeling sophisticated. The location was about as rustic as it gets: a corrugated iron shed on an outback farm. I did the complete styling, using earthy colours and natural textures in keeping with the garden theme. For the décor, I ended up emptying my entire potting shed at home and rustling up some of the contents of my house. My friends from *Provincial Home Living* provided us with furniture.

The ceiling was decked with wicker light fittings and green hanging ferns. On the guest tables, I featured small terracotta pots of herbs and ferns on a custom-designed garden-print tablecloth. For the centrepiece of the bridal table, on the other hand, I chose lily of the valley. The juxtaposition of all the informal elements with this most elegant and decadent of flowers created an air of unpretentious opulence.

OLIVE TREES
AND BAY
LEAVES

It might sound strange, but I think I was Greek in a past life. In fact, I know I was, because when a gorgeous Greek bride-to-be walked through the door of my studio, I felt an immediate connection to her and her family.

This consultation was the beginning of a beautiful friendship. In the lead-up to the wedding, all the female members of the family came together to make the mini planters for the baby olive trees, which each wedding guest would take home. To make the planters, we wrapped rolls of plaster from the craft shop around paper cups. We then filled each vessel with a bit of soil and a tiny olive sapling. Those weekends were filled with laughter, incredible food and flowing wine.

The wedding was held at a venue in an old timber yard. Located down a nondescript street, it was cavernous in size, with exposed wooden beams and beautiful wood pieces strewn throughout the space. It was bursting with warmth and character.

This wedding was the perfect combination of everything I love: the simplicity of the green-and-white design, guelder roses, Queen Anne's lace, sweet pea, andromeda and garlands of bay leaves winding down the length of each table.

Huge lopped tree branches were hung from the ceiling to create a textured leafy green canopy.

It's no accident either that the olive tree is the ancient Greek symbol for peace and friendship…

BLUSH
WEDDING

This was a beautiful, elegant wedding to match the couple who walked through my studio doors early last year. I designed and created a romantic garden wedding in hues of blush and white with orchids, South American roses, hellebores, blossom, scabious, ranunculus and touches of green foliage.

With stunning crystal-cut vessels and crystal candle-holders radiating an abundance of soft candlelight throughout the room, this wedding was simply gorgeous.

CHRISTMAS

For me, Christmas is a northern hemisphere tradition and must be celebrated as such. I don't care if it's 30 degrees and you're on a balcony overlooking Sydney Harbour – you better not even think about serving me seafood (my sister found this out the hard way!). Christmas dinner for my family is *always*: turkey and ham with bread sauce and redcurrant jam, followed by plum pudding with proper French-brandy butter.

The Scandinavians know how to do Christmas decorating with real style. They understand that green and white should make up the main elements, with just a hint of red to draw the eye to the focal point. I think it's so elegant to decorate a Christmas tree with nothing but fairy lights – a stack of beautifully wrapped presents underneath adding the only touch of colour.

My Christmas arrangements, whether for clients or my own home, are always clean and sparse in the Nordic style. I like to use masses of green spruce or pine foliage (no flowers or decorations!) for wreaths, vase arrangements and table centrepieces. I'll add buckets and baskets of pine cones around the place, set a few simple candles on the mantelpiece, and wrap all the presents in matching paper. Our family Christmas tree is decorated with antique glass and painted wooden ornaments in muted colours, creating an old-world atmosphere and adding to the sense of tradition.

ACKNOWLEDGEMENTS

I'd like to thank my tireless, funny, amazing, creative and hysterical team of florists. Without you, my endless days and nights would be very quiet, to say the least. To my loyal suppliers: thank you all for your continued support. To the amazing community that is the events industry in Australia and all the people I have worked with for so many years: thank you for continuing to keep our industry relevant. To my family – my husband Lock and my children Milly and Archie, and Mum and Dad: thank you for continuing to support me throughout this lifelong journey. Lastly, thank you to all my incredibly loyal clients, many of whom have become friends. Your ongoing support has been overwhelming and is my motivation to continue everyday.

Select photographs courtesy of:

Elisendra Russell
Erin & Tara
Gloss Creative
Jessie Brinkman Evans
Kara Rosenlund
Kirsty Macafee
Lisa Cohen
Molly Cusack
Red Rabbit Photography
Sam Bisso

All other photos in this book
were taken on an iPhone by Fleur McHarg.

FLEUR

Fleur McHarg has been creating glorious and unique floral arrangements for over 25 years. With an unparalleled instinct for colour and endless creative conceptions, Fleur has designed for events in Australia and internationally. Her work has been featured in magazines including *Vogue* Mexico and *Vogue Living* Australia.

Front cover image: Sam Bisso
Back cover image: Anthea Nicoll / Red Rabbit Photography

Design: Evi O Studio

Editing and additional material: Jessica Redman

The Flower Expert copyright © 2018 Thames & Hudson
Text copyright © 2018 Fleur McHarg
Images copyright © remains with the individual copyrights holders

First published in 2018 in hardcover in the United States of
America by Thames & Hudson Inc., 500 Fifth Avenue, New York,
New York 10110

thamesandhudsonusa.com

Library of Congress Catalog Card Number: 2018941606

ISBN 978-0-500-50124-5

Printed and bound in China by 1010.